Horse Chinese Horoscope 2024

By
IChingHun FengShuisu

*Copyright © 2024 By IChingHun FengShuisu
All rights reserved*

Table of Contents

Introduce 5
Year of the HORSE (Water) | (1942) & (2002) 7
   Overview 7
   Career and Business 9
   Financial 10
   Family 11
   Love 12
   Health 13
Year of the HORSE (Wood) | (1954) & (2014) 15
   Overview 15
   Career and Business 17
   Financial 18
   Family 19
   Love 20
   Health 21
Year of the HORSE (Fire) | (1966) 23
   Overview 23
   Career and Business 25
   Financial 26
   Family 27
   Love 28
   Health 29
Year of the HORSE (Earth) | (1978) 30
   Overview 30
   Career and Business 32
   Financial 33
   Family 34

Love	35
Health	36
**Year of the HORSE (Gold)	(1990)**	36
Overview	37
Career and Business	38
Financial	39
Family	40
Love	41
Health	42
Chinese Astrology Horoscope for Each Month	44
Month 12 in the Rabbit Year (6 Jan 23 - 3 Feb 23)	44
Month 1 in the Dragon Year (4 Feb 23 - 5 Mar 23)	46
Month 2 in the Dragon Year (6 Mar 23 - 5 Apr 23)	48
Month 3 in the Dragon Year (6 Apr 23 - 5 May 23)	50
Month 4 in the Dragon Year (6 May 23 - 5 Jun 23)	52
Month 5 in the Dragon Year (6 Jun 23 - 6 Jul 23)	54
Month 6 in the Dragon Year (7 Jul 23 - 7 Aug 23)	56
Month 7 in the Dragon Year (8 Aug 23 - 7 Sep 23)	59
Month 8 in the Dragon Year (8 Sep 23 - 7 Oct 23)	61
Month 9 in the Dragon Year (8 Oct 23 - 6 Nov 23)	63
Month 10 in the Dragon Year (7 Nov 23 - 6 Dec 23)	65
Month 11 in the Dragon Year (7 Dec 23 - 5 Jan 24)	67
Amulet for The Year of the Horse	70

Introduce

The character of people born in the year of the HORSE

People born this year like to talk, talk wisely, and have a lot of patience. You can endure any problem, no matter how difficult it is, without complaining in front of others. You enjoy making the best use of your physical strength. When you want something, you usually do it yourself unless you have lofty goals. Hardworking, not passive, always alert, enjoys being the center of attention, enjoys attending social events, participates in almost all sports, enjoys traveling, and enjoys competition. You are self-centered, despise conventions, and are cunning rather than clever. People born in this year value freedom, dislike being forced to do things they don't want to do, and are willing to give up everything for love.

Strength:
You get along well with others and are respected by them, brave.

Weaknesses:

You have a bad temper and frequently cause harm to others for no reason.

Love:
This year's babies are very attractive. Their love is not showy, but it is constant. It could be said that there are people who come almost every day to flirt and say nice things, and who would like others to come and take care of them. People born in this year dislike inconsistent people. A good-looking person with a narcissistic personality, on the other hand, is constantly thinking about how handsome or beautiful you are. People born in this year believe that they must be the only ones, so if you enjoy being pampered, you can be confident that you can permanently bind your lover.

Suitable Career:
People born in the Year of the Horse are fire-elemental, so they should pursue a career that matches their destiny, and their ability to promote progress, prosperity, and profit. Education, research, occupation, teacher,

doctor, administrator, beautician, gas station, photographer, shop selling stationery, all types of electrical equipment or handicrafts, selling artificial flowers, selling cloth, selling drugs, and creating publishing houses are all careers that will suit your luck. It was fated for you to be born in the Year of the Horse.

Year of the HORSE (Water) | (1942) & (2002)

"The Horse that Travels " is a person born in the year of the HORSE at the age of 82 years (1942) and 23 years (2002)

Overview

For young people born in the Year of the Horse around the age of 22, your horoscope for this year indicates that money, fortune, and auspiciousness will visit you. Take advantage of the lucky periods in the months that will help you this year. Increase your diligence, learn new things, and grow as a person. Whether it's taking on a large project, developing a portfolio, or stepping out to establish yourself as your boss. Because this year's omens for both labor and business are considered good. As a result, you must strengthen your bravery, dare to go forward and hunt for chances. Dare to do large things, and dare to work hard. Because it is a prosperous period, we should take the first step toward our objective. But, throughout the year, wicked stars "Bua Sing" and "Dao Kuang Sa" circle to disturb and disturb. It will have ramifications for your health and the safety of others in your household. Be wary of unanticipated current costs that might lead to a lack of cash. When a group of people congregate to stroll around, be careful not to be caught in the crossfire and do injury. Both groups of friends this year must be able to discriminate. Take caution not to be duped into getting into trouble. You might get in trouble, be sued, or even go to jail.

Because the planets that orbit into your zodiac sign are "Dao Bua Sing" this year, senior horoscopes must attempt to take excellent care of their health. Be especially cautious of disorders that cause discomfort and necessitate frequent visits to medical institutions. Senior citizens, on the other hand, should make time to pay reverence to the Buddha to alleviate misfortune. Also, avoid interfering in your children's affairs. If you have the chance, you should make time to produce merit, generate merit, provide alms, and save animals' lives. It will make you feel more at ease and happy. You should keep your mood clear and let go of any issues that develop for your bodily and mental well-being.

Career and Business

This year's work is regarded well. You must, however, exercise caution. You must be persistent to obtain it. It wasn't only a gift from God. However, you should use your knowledge and ability to produce visible outcomes. As a result, no matter what task you undertake, you should do it properly and with integrity. Adults will be relied on to assist. If you own a firm, you need to evaluate the market regularly, contact clients, and understand how to build marketing and goods. Which will encourage you to move to the next level. During the month that the work and business of the destined person in both life cycles experience good progress and prosperity, namely the 1st Chinese month (4 Feb. - 4 Mar.), 6th Chinese month (6 Jul. - 6 Aug.), 8th Chinese month (7 Sep. - 7 Oct.) and 9th Chinese month (8 Oct. - 6 Nov.). Months where work will be disrupted and encounter problems include the 12th Chinese month (6 Jan. - 3 Feb.), the 2nd Chinese month (5 Mar. - 3 Apr.), the 5th Chinese month (5 Jun. – 5 Jul.), and the 11th month of China (6 Dec. 2024 – 4 Jan. 2025), be careful of falling into the trap of criminals who will trick you into losing your wealth.

Financial

The fate owner's financial wealth swings considerably. Even this year, you might receive money unexpectedly. However, if you are greedy or irresponsible, you have the right to lose everything. Financial planning is thus required, and you should take care of the liquidity of your working capital to avoid company stagnation difficulties. You should also avoid doing business with those who are likely to break the law. Otherwise, you will become entangled in the web and suffer as well.

Especially during the months when your finances will be depressed, including the 12th Chinese month (6 Jan. - 3 Feb.), the 2nd Chinese month (5 Mar. - 3 Apr.), the 5th Chinese month (5 Jun. – 5 Jul.), and the 11th Chinese month (6 Dec. 2024 – 4 Jan. 2025) Gambling is not permitted. Do not show your affection for a buddy by lending money on his or her behalf, giving money to a friend, or signing financial guarantees for a friend out of regard. Because this might result in shared culpability in a legal proceeding or property damage. For the months in which your finances are flowing smoothly, including the 1st Chinese month (4 Feb. - 4 Mar.), the 6th Chinese month (6 Jul. - 6 Aug.), the 8th Chinese month (7 Sep. – 7 Oct.), and the 9th Chinese month (8 Oct. – 6 Nov.)

Family

This year's horoscope for your family has good energy. It will motivate you to develop guidelines for managing auspicious work in your house. There is a chance to welcome new members to the home. It is a good time to move into a new home or apartment. You should not, however, underestimate the bad force that emanates from the unfavorable constellations that you focus on. Both the evil stars "Buang Sing" and "Kuang Sao" frequently cause difficulties that cause you to lose money and incur medical bills. When providing first aid in the house, you must pay special attention to the safety of family members. That may encounter unexpected events, especially during the 12th Chinese month (6 Jan. - 3 Feb.), the 2nd Chinese month (5 Mar. - 3 Apr.), the 5th Chinese month (5 Jun. – 5 July), and the 11th month of China (6 Dec. 2024 – 4 Jan. 25) You should be more cautious about misplacing or stealing items from your house, as well as causing health concerns or accidents.

Love

The love horoscope for this year appears to favor singles. For those of you who have been together a long time and believe that this person is the one. You may start planning your wedding dress this year. Set an auspicious day now, or for those of you who are still in the process of creating a connection and wish to move from friends to close friends. Let's hurry up and score this year so we can keep going back and forth. The love tree will soon bloom as planned. There's a potential for wedding bells to sound. Because this year is an opportune period for proposing, becoming engaged, marrying, or marrying. However, you should be careful during the months when love problems will occur, including the 12th Chinese month (6 Jan. - 3 Feb.), the 2nd Chinese month (5 Mar. - 3 Apr.), the 5th Chinese month (5 Jun - 5 Jul) and the 11th Chinese month (6 Dec 2024 - 4 Jan 2025). Be wary of disagreements and disputes. Do not meddle with other spouses' intimate ties. You should also avoid going to places of amusement. Because it will just produce problems and sickness.

Health
The Lord Destiny's health in both life cycles is good this year. For the fate of teens since it is a vibrant age. As a result, capable of battling hard effort. But don't take your own and your family's safety for granted. Furthermore, if you join a group to walk around, be aware that you may have disagreements with other groups, causing you to become entangled in the net and maybe commit a crime. For the months when

your destiny and age assessments should be more cautious and concerned with your health and safety, including the 12th Chinese month (6 Jan. - 3 Feb.), the 2nd Chinese month (5 Mar. - 3 Apr.), 5th Chinese month (5 Jun. - 5 Jul.) and 11th Chinese month (6 Dec. 2023 - 4 Jan. 2024), You should be extra cautious regarding workplace and automobile accidents.

Year of the HORSE (Wood) | (1954) & (2014)

"The HORSE in the grass " is a person born in the year of the HORSE at the age of 70 years (1954) and 10 years (2014)

Overview

This year is a fortunate year for seniors over the age of 70 in general. As a result, it is appropriate to pick heirs, children, or assistance to assist with the task. Prepare to work as a representative for you in the future. Work and company will benefit from patronage this year. As a result, work will progress, and business will grow and thrive. But since this year's planets in your house of destiny are Buang Sing, Nine Satellite, and Kuang Sao. As a result, each step you take must be carefully considered. This is due to three negative stars affecting the house of Destiny. This frequently expands its impact, resulting in disagreements and arguments both within and beyond the organization. As a result, this year you should use the concepts of effective personnel management, such as placing individuals in the correct roles and allowing people in the same group to work together, rather than establishing units where there is just disagreement and no need to go forward. If you must modify and transfer work duties, make certain that the transferred individual is not disappointed. Because it will diminish productivity. Then there's your personal health issue. Diabetes, high blood pressure, food poisoning, stress, poor sleep, and poor food hygiene should all be avoided. By avoiding foods that are overly sweet, salty, or greasy, because sickness is caused by diet. This year, you should avoid or limit hot food categories, as well as other grilled, grilled, and fried dishes.

The planet that will enter its zodiac sign this year is known as the "Buying Sing Star" for young people of this age. This star's influence causes many things to go wrong this year. You should be more diligent than ever before when it comes to learning and studying. Don't be reckless about trying new things, especially traveling. There will be an accident, so be cautious.

Career and Business

This year's work, including commercial activity, should be done soon. Don't be frightened to remain calm and relaxed. The artwork will be harmed. This year, the most essential issue to focus on is people management. Protests will erupt if poor management is not addressed. As a result, work becomes stalled and does not flow smoothly. Especially during the months when work and business will be disrupted and encounter problems, including the 12th Chinese month (6 Jan. - 3 Feb.), the 2nd Chinese month (5 Mar. - 3 Apr.), and the 5th Chinese month. (5 Jun – 5 Jul) and the 11th Chinese month (6 Dec. 2024 – 4 Jan. 2025) Be wary of failing to provide work on time due to interference that causes harm. Making an employment contract or hiring someone can be deceived into improving the correctness of contract terms. Furthermore, you should not increase your investment because you might be duped.

For the month of work, the education and investments of the destined people in both life cycles have a bright and prosperous direction, including the 1st Chinese month (4 Feb. - 4 Mar.), the 6th Chinese month (6 Jul. - 6 Aug.), 8th Chinese month (7 Sep. – 7 Oct.) and 9th Chinese month (8 Oct. – 6 Nov.).

Financial

This year's work, including commercial activity, should be done soon. Don't be frightened to remain calm and relaxed. The artwork will be harmed. This year, the most essential issue to focus on is people management. Protests will erupt if poor management is not addressed. As a result, work becomes stalled and does not flow smoothly. Especially during the months when work and business will be disrupted and encounter problems, including the 12th Chinese month (6 Jan. - 3 Feb.), the 2nd Chinese month (5 Mar. - 3 Apr.), and the 5th Chinese month. (5 Jun – 5 Jul) and the 11th Chinese month (6 Dec. 2024 – 4 Jan. 2025) Be wary of failing to provide work on time due to interference that causes harm. Making an employment contract or hiring someone can be deceived into improving the correctness of contract terms. Furthermore, you should not increase your investment because you might be duped.

For the month of work, the education and investments of the destined people in both life cycles have a bright and prosperous direction, including the 1st Chinese month (4 Feb. - 4 Mar.), the 6th Chinese month (6 Jul. - 6 Aug.), 8th Chinese month (7 Sep. – 7 Oct.) and 9th Chinese month (8 Oct. – 6 Nov.).

Family

This year's family horoscope for the Lord of Destiny in both life cycles is a combination of good and evil. Even if there is an auspicious power of patronage, it will convey good news about the success of the individuals in the house, or there may be conditions for conducting auspicious activities. However, as a result of being influenced by the evil constellation, its effect expands as well. Both the Sing and Nine Tiangs stars create things that you should be cautious of. Health issues for you and others in your house, illness of youngsters or the elderly, be cautious of safety in your home, danger of harm, bleeding from accidents, problems with disagreements, conflicts among individuals within. The months in which there will be chaos in your family include the 12th Chinese month (6 Jan. - 3 Feb.), the 2nd Chinese month (5 Mar. - 3 Apr.), the 5th Chinese month (5 June - 5 July), and the 11th Chinese month (6 Dec. '24 - 4 Jan. '25) During this time, be extra cautious about the risk of losing your goods to criminals or neglect. Be extra cautious about water hazards for youngsters at this time. As a result, you should avoid swimming in public locations and avoid traveling by water.

Love

This year has been quite dreary and frigid in terms of love. Perhaps it's because they've been together for so long. You both know one other so well that the absence of taste makes your love feel indifferent; being near to you feels far away. Don't let the issue die because each side is unwilling to lose face. You might be better off taking a step back and letting things go. Closing one eye might assist you in avoiding becoming angry in particular situations. Especially during the months when relationships are quite fragile and easy to cause quarrels, namely the 12th Chinese month (6 Jan. - 3 Feb.), the 2nd Chinese month (5 Mar. - 3 Apr.), 5th Chinese month (5 Jun. - 5 Jul.) and 11th Chinese months (6 Dec 2024 - 4 Jan. 2025) should be careful and know how to act like an adult, don't accidentally get involved with temporary love when you are old and you should avoid going to entertainment venues.

Health

This year's health is not looking good. You should be cautious about hidden diseases attacking elders or previous ailments reappearing. Diabetes and excessive blood pressure, which can induce dizziness and headaches, should also be avoided. You must be cautious while wandering around, and you may get bruises, bleeding, or infectious infections as a result of eating anything you want. In addition to allergies, seasonal epidemics, and accidents from activities outside the house, we must be particularly cautious of water risks for small children this year during the terrible months. During the months that fateful people in both life cycles must take extra care of their health and be especially careful about safety, including the 12th Chinese month (6 Jan. - 3 Feb.), the 2nd Chinese month (5 Mar. - 3 Apr.), the 5th Chinese month(5 Jun – 5 Jul) and 11th Chinese month (6 Dec. 2024 – 4 Jan. 2025).

Year of the HORSE (Fire) | (1966)

"The Horse in Stall" is a person born in the year of the HORSE at the age of 58 years (1966)

Overview

The planets that circle into the house of destiny and disseminate their impact on you this year, the Singing Star, are responsible for the fate criterion for individuals born in the Year of the Horse around the age of 58. Although your life cycle will gain power this year as a whole. An auspicious visit will inspire you to achieve fame, honor, status, and a great deal of money. Furthermore, the family base obtained patronage power to aid support. The Lord of Destiny will have the option to purchase pricey real estate this year. Moving into a new house or habitation will be an auspicious occasion. There are conditions in the house for planning more auspicious gatherings. You may open a store, a branch, or a new factory, or you might invest in a new firm. As previously planned the aim or selecting to enter the capital market by buying stock exchange shares or buying shares to acquire a firm (takeover) at a favorable period of this year. Many goods will receive positive reviews.

Finances are fairly good in terms of good fortune. You have the option of investing both domestically and outside. Dividends are expected to be paid. During the year, however, one should not overlook the wicked stars that circle and upset both the Bua Sing and Kuang Sao stars. Which will have an immediate influence on health. When drinking and eating, you should practice good hygiene. As an aged person, you should avoid eating meals that are overly salty or sugary. Food should be diverse and well-balanced. You should also be aware of persons in the household's blood pressure, heart disease, and blood-related ailments and health concerns. Next, you must use caution in the event of an accident. You should be cautious of leg injuries or mishaps that cause blood to flow. As a result, you must use extreme caution when working and driving.

Career and Business

The work of this year is the criterion for gaining both money and renown. However, you should search for heirs, children, or assistance to help you stretch your wings as arms and legs. Whether it's raising funds or buying target stocks with a bright future. You should consider investing in equities connected to raw materials, commodities, energy, oil, and natural gas, all of which have the potential to generate profits for you. But you should be careful during the 12th Chinese month (6 Jan. - 3 Feb.), the 2nd Chinese month (5 Mar. - 3 Apr.), the 5th Chinese month (5 Jun. - 5 Jul. .), and the 11th month of China (6 Dec. '24 - 4 Jan. '25) during this period, be careful of external economic fluctuations. It will affect you in many parts. Be careful of subordinates causing problems. In addition, when making any contract, you should read the minutiae carefully. Be careful of being at a disadvantage. As for the months in which your work and business will experience success and prosperity, they are the 1st Chinese month (4 Feb. - 4 Mar.), the 6th Chinese month (6 Jul. - 6 Aug.), 8th Chinese month (7

Sep. – 7 Oct.) and 9th Chinese month (8 Oct. – 6 Nov.).

Financial

This year, your finances are highly volatile throughout the months when money comes in. You must actively conserve and protect your assets. As a result, when confronted with a financial downturn, income drops costs follow in the shadows, and money is not spent until it becomes too stressful. This year, financial issues will produce debt stress and leakage points, perhaps resulting in a shortage of liquidity. You should also be wary of sudden greed, as investing incorrectly might result in asset loss. You should also be cautious of debtors' accounts where bad debts may be discovered or collected with difficulty. Especially during the 12th Chinese month (6 Jan. - 3 Feb.), the 2nd Chinese month (5 Mar. - 3 Apr.), the 5th Chinese month (5 Jun. - 5 Jul.) and the 11th Chinese month (6 Dec. 2024 - 4 Jan. 2025) should keep a tight eye on working capital liquidity. Don't lend money or sign financial assurances. Stop gambling. Don't invest in illicit firms since you could be caught.

Furthermore, many investments must be avoided. Because there is a danger that they will be duped and lose money. As for the months where finances are flowing smoothly, they are the 1st Chinese month (4 Feb. - 4 Mar.), the 6th Chinese month (6 Jul. - 6 Aug.), the 8th Chinese month (7 Sep. – 7 Oct.) and the 9th Chinese month (8 Oct. – 6 Nov.)

Family

This year's horoscope for your family is not favorable. This is because during the year, groups of bad stars, such as the Bua Sing and Diao Sing stars, will come to annoy you. As a result, the first thing you should be concerned about is the health of the members of the home. The second issue is house safety, which includes fixtures, tools, electrical appliances, and gas burners. They should always be inspected to guarantee their safety. If a part is determined to be damaged, it should be fixed or replaced as soon as possible. Especially during the 12th Chinese month (6 Jan. - 3 Feb.), the 2nd Chinese month (5 Mar. - 3 Apr.), the 5th Chinese month (5 Jun. - 5 Jul.), and the 11th Chinese month (6 Dec. 2024 - 4 Jan. 2025) during this period, be careful of mourning for elderly relatives and be careful of valuables being damaged, lost or stolen.

Love

This year, the love of your destiny will encounter both good and negative things. A tough heart may recognize that when you are joyful, your mind will appear happy and cheerful. When you are psychologically miserable, you wither and become dissatisfied with everything. To stay in the groove this year, you need to take care of your head. Don't be overly explosive and preoccupied, hurling your emotions at those near you. If you wish to sweeten your romantic connection. Take your loved one on a sightseeing tour or make offerings to the monks at the monastery when you have spare time. It will make your mind feel better. However, you should be careful during the following months when love is quite fragile and arguments can easily occur: the 12th Chinese month (6 Jan. - 3 Feb.), the 2nd Chinese month (5 Mar. - 3 Apr.), the 5th Chinese month (5 Jun. - 5 Jul.) and 11th Chinese month (6 Dec. 67 - 4 Jan. 68) Do not interfere in the relationships of other couples and refrain from wandering around in nighttime entertainment venues.

Health

Your health is suffering as a result of the wicked constellations' influence. As a result, you should be cautious of silent diseases that appear to cause sickness. You should be cautious about high blood pressure. Shortness of breath, heart illness, and signs of blood not reaching the brain in time, resulting in fainting and dizziness. Be cautious about falling and damaging your legs, especially if you frequently get knee pain and body pains. However, if you have the impression that anything is awry this year. You should visit a doctor very early for an accurate diagnosis and treatment. For the months in which you need to pay more attention to your health, including the 12th Chinese month (6 Jan. - 3 Feb.), the 2nd Chinese month (5 Mar. - 3 Apr.), the 5th Chinese month (5 Jun - 5 Jul) and the 11th Chinese month (6 Dec. 2024 - 4 Jan. 2025) to be more careful about accidents both during work and travel.

Year of the HORSE (Earth) | (1978)

" The horse in the stable " is a person born in the year of the HORSE at the age of 46 years (1978)

Overview

Lord, the fate of the Horse Year is about this age. This year is regarded to be an auspicious year since the planet that circles into your house of destiny this year is the "Kuang Sao" star. Your career will advance, and your company will grow to the point where you may start your firm, create further branches, construct new stores, develop extra factories, or invest in other enterprises. External investment, both investing in and acquiring equities, is heading in the right way. There will be a chance to purchase the appropriate item at the right moment and sell it at a profit, or if you purchase and keep it, you will earn a pleasing dividend. However, the presence of wicked stars coming to disturb and disturb, particularly "Dao Kuang Sao" and "Dao Xiaoying," would have a significant influence on the loss of riches in unforeseen circumstances during the year. Work should be completed peacefully. Do not be impatient since if you make a mistake, you may lose money from ordering and accepting work.

You should speak clearly with the opposite party this year. Otherwise, it might harm the job and result in losses. You will also discover that debtors' accounts are bad debts, and you will be afraid of dealing with government authorities, being audited, or being searched and evading penalty.

You should be cautious regarding family safety within the home. When installing objects, you must check for strength regularly. If it is damaged, it should be fixed or replaced as soon as possible. You should also be cautious about fires, and various electrical devices and gas burners should be properly examined. Be cautious of intruders breaking into your house. In terms of love, you must be aware of and regulate your own heart this year. Don't let your guard down. Because of the foundation of your love, you will meet the wicked star this year, who will spew venom at you, causing quarrels. Family strife is being caused by a family feud.

Career and Business

This year's job will be fraught with difficulties. There will be issues in business. What you should do is carry out your responsibilities to the best of your abilities. Do not meddle with other people's jobs. Develop and maintain positive connections with individuals at all levels. Be wary of persons who do not intend to defame you in private. We're in big trouble. The work should be simple. Especially during the months when your work and business often encounter obstacles and problems, such as during the 12th Chinese month (6 Jan. - 3 Feb.), the 2nd Chinese month (5 Mar. - 3 Apr.), the 5th Chinese month (5 Jun - 5 Jul) and the 11th Chinese month (6 Dec 2024 - 4 Jan 2025). Be careful of being transferred and changed positions. Be careful of making promises. You may be tricked into causing damage and disadvantage. As for the months when work and business are prosperous, they include the 1st Chinese month (4 Feb. - 4 Mar.), the 6th Chinese month (6 Jul. - 6 Aug.), the 8th Chinese month (7 Sep. – 7 Oct.) and the 9th Chinese month (8 Oct. – 6 Nov.).

Financial

This year's earnings are sufficient financially. But be careful with money from fortune because once you get it, you will not be able to stop. In the end, more people will be recalled for behaviors such as evading taxes, breaking the law, or violating the copyrights of others. Be wary of getting audited and probed for past concerns this year. You may face significant penalties or be unable to avoid criminal accusations. During the months when the financial star is in decline and you have to be careful of being checked by legal officials, it will cause you to lose your assets, including the 12th Chinese month (6 Jan. - 3 Feb.), the 2nd Chinese month (5 Mar. - 3 Apr.), 5th Chinese month (5 Jun. - 5 Jul.) and 11th Chinese month (6 Dec. 2024 - 4 Jan. 2025). Be wary of the wicked star Guang Sao's influence. It will generate temporary greed, and you may lose your fortune without recognizing it. You should also avoid gambling and having unanticipated circumstances occur that lead you to lose a substantial chunk of money, resulting in a lack of liquidity in your finances. As for the months that support and encourage your finances to flow smoothly, they are the 1st Chinese month (4 Feb. - 4 Mar.), the 6th Chinese month (6 Jul. - 6 Aug.), the 8th Chinese month (7 Sep. - 7 Oct.) and the 9th Chinese month (8 Oct. - 6 Nov.)

Family

The family horoscope for this year is troubling. It was due to the Evil Star Guang Sao and the Xiao Ying Star that had orbited to invade. You frequently generate dangers and have an impact on the safety of your house. Be cautious; the invader may cause unanticipated violence to anyone in the residence. Be wary of criminals taking your goods or individuals in your neighborhood arguing with neighbors. The nice friendship that previously existed is destroyed. Increase your vigilance and take better care of your house, especially during the 12th Chinese month (6 Jan. - 3 Feb.), the 2nd Chinese month (5 Mar. - 3 Apr.), the 5th Chinese month (5 Jun. - 5 Jul.), and the 11th Chinese month (6 Dec. 2024 - 4 Jan. 2025). You are responsible for safety and urge everyone in the family not to argue or argue, and to be cautious of accidents.

Love

Your connection with your spouse is not easy when it comes to love. Some frequent quarrels and disagreements harm one another. This year, avoid nasty gossip. Premature menopause can induce irritation and changes in speech and behavior. It will exacerbate the conflict if it is on both sides. As a result, you should turn around calmly and talk politely. It's preferable to retaliating and lecturing each other, which will only make matters worse. Especially during the 12th Chinese month (6 Jan. - 3 Feb.), the 2nd Chinese month (5 Mar. - 3 Apr.), the 5th Chinese month (5 Jun - 5 Jul.), and the 11th Chinese month (6 Dec 2024 - 4 Jan 2025), when you should avoid getting involved with other people's family members. Avoid visiting places of entertainment that may expose you to sickness.

Health

This year, your overall health is mediocre. However, his health deteriorated and he got feeble in the middle of the year. Be cautious if you are easily allergic to the air, frequently have colds, or have headaches or dizziness, and be aware that taking cold medicine can make you drowsy, so you should avoid any job that requires equipment or driving. Because an accident is very likely. Especially during the 12th Chinese month (6 Jan. - 3 Feb.), the 2nd Chinese month (5 Mar. - 3 Apr.), the 5th Chinese month (5 Jun. - 5 Jul.), and the 11th Chinese month (6 Dec. 2024 - 4 Jan. 2025) You should constantly be cautious and mindful of your food and living habits. You should also be cautious of accidents when working or driving, as well as the possibility of injury and bleeding.

Year of the HORSE (Gold) | (1990)

" The Horse In the Sky" is a person born in the year of the HORSE at the age of 34 years (1990)

Overview

The planet that orbits into your destiny home this year is the Bua Sing star for those born in the Year of the Horse. Overall, this year is thought to be another favorable moment for you to meet a benefactor. Your career will advance. The commercial firm can grow by adding new branches, goods, and services, and you may invest in, join, or acquire stocks that interest you through the stock exchange or directly. They will all make progress and bear blooms and fruits. This year's family horoscope predicts the possibility of purchasing pricey real estate. There is also a lucky time to move into a new home or apartment. This year, however, may you be resolute and daring in your pursuit of success for yourself. Diligence and intelligence will ensure that the task is done correctly and that it is appealing to consumers or those receiving services, as well as superiors. But since evil stars were whirling about and bothering both the Nine Third Evil Star and the Snaking Star during the year in the house of fate. This set of stars will have a detrimental impact on both you and your family. It will produce a variety of issues, including accidents, health issues for family members, conflicts, and legal issues. The occurrence of unexpected events causes loss of property.

Career and Business

Even if there will be a favorable moment for expansion, this year's work is a criterion to be sure before taking action. However, if there is a lack of planning and preparation in all matters, the chances of success are reduced. You must not, in particular, overlook the importance of cultivating positive connections both inside and outside the agency by visiting and enquiring about the well-being of those with whom you frequently interact. It will allow you the authority to favor in any way to climb to a higher position. Especially during the months when your business and business are prosperous and progressing well, namely the 1st Chinese month (4 Feb. - 4 Mar.), the 6th Chinese month (6 Jul. - 6 Aug.), the 8th Chinese month. (7 Sep. - 7 Oct.) and the 9th Chinese month (8 Oct. - 6 Nov.) for the months when work and business will be stuck and encounter problems, including the 12th Chinese month (6 Jan. – 3 Feb.), 2nd Chinese month (5 Mar. – 3 Apr.), 5th Chinese month (5 Jun. – 5 Jul), and 11th Chinese month (6 Dec. 2024 – 4 Jan. 2025) You must avoid being obstructed both inwardly and outside. When signing any contract paperwork, read them carefully, be wary of terms that may exploit you, and be wary of fraudsters who will deceive you with exaggeratedly attractive illusions. You will become a victim and harm if you are duped.

Financial

This year's salary is fairly nice financially. However, there will be times when there will be conditions for obtaining a lump payment. You must use caution while dealing with money from fortune. Don't be greedy and overinvest. You should be mindful of how you manage your working capital. Because there may be unanticipated fluctuations from external events that will affect you. Investing in some categories will have an impact and create harm. As a result, selling some equities risks leaving them or accepting losses initially. Perhaps it will be less painful. Especially during the months when the financial stars are down, including the 12th Chinese month (6 Jan. - 3 Feb.), the 2nd Chinese month (5 Mar. - 3 Apr.), the 5th Chinese month (5 Jun. – 5 Jul), and the 11th Chinese month (6 Dec. 2024 – 4 Jan. 2025) You must take care of your liquidity by refraining from lending money, signing guarantees, gambling, taking risks, and engaging in illegal activity, as well as keeping an eye out for litigation and disputes with government authorities. In terms of the month, money will be in order. You will have good fortune for several months, including the 1st Chinese month (4 Feb. - 4 Mar.), the 6th Chinese month (6 Jul. - 6 Aug.), the 8th Chinese month (7 Sep. – 7 Oct.) and the 9th Chinese month (8 Oct. – 6 Nov.)

Family

This year's family horoscope will have both pleasant and bad aspects. Although there are times when you will experience favorable patronage powers. There is excellent news and accomplishments to cheer about in the home. However, you will be impacted by the wicked stars that spread their effect. The dangerous planet and the celestial dog both cause the natives to be reckless in dealing with it. Specifically, the elderly's health at home and the safety of family members. Be cautious since unexpected incidents will occur. For the months when troubles will occur in your family, these are the 12th Chinese month (6 Jan. - 3 Feb.), the 2nd Chinese month (5 Mar. - 3 Apr.), the 5th Chinese month (5 Jun - 5 Jul) and the 11th Chinese month (6 Dec. 2024 - 4 Jan. 2025) should be more cautious about domestic disputes. Be wary of squandering money on medical bills for family members, as well as robbers stealing into your home.

Love

The love of this year's destiny is not smooth, and it will easily cause storms to collide. You must exercise caution in controlling your emotions so that they do not erupt. Because otherwise, the road will only lead to brokenness. Especially during the months when your love is fragile and problems can easily occur, such as the 12th Chinese month (6 Jan. - 3 Feb.), the 2nd Chinese month (5 Mar. - 3 Apr.) Chinese 5th month (5 Jun - 5 Jul) and Chinese 11th month (6 Dec 2024 - 4 Jan 2025). Avoid becoming engaged in other people's family difficulties. Be wary of third persons who may get dangerously near to producing misunderstandings, or you should calm down. During this period, be aware of anyone who claims to befriend you. If you make a mistake, it will lead to a slew of issues. Furthermore, avoid going to entertainment locations to avoid catching sickness.

Health

This year's fate's health is a criterion for monitoring. Because he encountered the demon Tom Huai by chance and launched a wave of strength to unsettle him. As a consequence, you must avoid vices like alcohol and drugs, as well as traveling, playing, and being cautious of accidents both at work and on the road, as well as "Dao Huai Yim," which may lead to damage, bleeding, and other ailments. This year, you may experience regular air allergies and develop colds easily, so focus on self-care and dietary hygiene. You should also avoid becoming ill or infected with seasonal epidemics. Causes illness, especially during the 12th Chinese month (6 Jan. - 3 Feb.), the 2nd Chinese month (5 Mar. - 3 Apr.), the 5th Chinese month (5 Jun. - 5 Sept. c.), and the 11th Chinese month (6 Dec. 2024 - 4 Jan. 2025).

Chinese Astrology Horoscope for Each Month

Month 12 in the Rabbit Year (6 Jan 23 - 3 Feb 23)

As for individuals born in the Year of the Horse, the start of the year this month has not yet reached the monsoon level. The horoscope's trajectory remains downward, while the surrounding clouds remain dismal and dim. However, please don't be too anxious during this time. Anything you can let go of would be beneficial. However, if certain issues are on the verge of becoming a catastrophe, you must act immediately and with integrity. You will be out of the monsoon zone by the middle of the month. If you plan to achieve progress in many professional activities during this period, you cannot be impatient since you will employ your emotions inadvertently. Be wary about offending clients or individuals you have to deal with, especially if you accidentally say anything improper. During this month, you should labor or negotiate on any topic that follows societal rules. Do not cross the line or seek methods to deceive. Otherwise, long-term difficulties will arise. As a result, you must work hard throughout this period.

Your financial wealth is moderate and on the decline. You should be wary of those that use profit figures to get you to invest. This labor will be well worth it. There are still challenges in the workplace. However, if you aim to repair it, you will be able to overcome the issue. Please strive to improve yourself. The good times are on their way. Those who improve themselves will be successful.

Even if you have some conflicts, average family horoscope, or love horoscope, you may communicate with each other. It will be better for you if you give in early. In terms of health, be wary of eye disorders like conjunctivitis, cataracts, heart disease, and seasonal infectious infections. You will be in a bloody mood with relatives and friends. You will almost certainly have quarrels and conflicts with your relatives. During this period, tell some things but don't divulge everything because if you trust them too much, you may lose your fortune, get into difficulty, and feel wounded.

Support Days: 3 Jan., 7 Jan., 11 Jan., 15 Jan., 19 Jan., 23 Jan., 27 Jan., 31 Jan.

Lucky Days: 8 Jan., 20 Jan.

Misfortune Days: 1 Jan., 13 Jan., 25 Jan.

Bad Days: 2 Jan., 4 Jan., 14 Jan., 16 Jan., 26 Jan., 28 Jan.

Month 1 in the Dragon Year (4 Feb 23 - 5 Mar 23)
The path of life for people born in the Year of the Horse this month will be uphill, even though their fate graph will be upward. As a consequence, while overall work has improved, there are still issues with sales and revenue that may not yet achieve the aim as expected in the commercial sector. You are regarded fortunate because auspicious stars will be circling you this month to strengthen you and relieve you from many binds. This month, you should go out and study the market regularly to determine the trend of client demand, and which items are popular, and go out and meet and chat with individuals you need to contact to visit or make friends with. Depending on

your abilities, including developing unity in the unit will strengthen the organization.

In terms of money, Dao Mongkol will encourage new investment options and channels that will provide the necessary advantages and profits. In terms of employment, you should continue to analyze the trade market this month to determine the best moment to invest in a new round or boost your investment in a new market. For the time being, your destiny should still be focused on preserving positive interpersonal relationships with people around you. Those with whom you must maintain continual touch to grow the outcomes of the trading market even more.

The power of patronage has arrived to visit the smooth family side. Members are still working well together. Love is still a wonderful thing. There are no severe ailments to bother us in terms of health. Good family and friends will provide assistance and support in beginning a new work. Joint partnerships and diverse investments will yield excellent results.

Support Days: 4 Feb., 8 Feb., 12 Feb., 16 Feb., 20 Feb., 24 Feb., 28 Feb.
Lucky Days: 1 Feb., 13 Feb., 25 Feb..
Misfortune Days: 6 Feb., 18 Feb.
Bad Days: 7 Feb., 9 Feb., 19 Feb., 21 Feb.

Month 2 in the Dragon Year (6 Mar 23 - 5 Apr 23)
Because it has moved to meet an adverse direction, the direction of your horoscope born in the Year of the Horse continues to vary up and down this month. You may go out and buy items you enjoy to heal bad luck at the beginning of the month, or you may take a portion of the money to make merit and produce merit. It will assist in mitigating the disaster. You should not meddle with other people's work throughout this month. Do your best in your obligations. Do not be arrogant or overbearing. Avoid getting hounded by annoying individuals who want to intimidate you.

In terms of financial fortune, the path is not clear. There will be an intervention, causing the money to contract. You must carefully handle your money throughout this period. Keep an eye out for a shortage of liquidity in the circulation system. No one should lend money or sign commitments, and no one should gamble. Do not engage in illicit activities, and be wary of robbers. The work side is experiencing monsoon conditions. Work and trade are hampered at the agency, leading to tensions. Be wary of clients fleeing to conduct business with other merchants, and be wary of troublemakers.

There is a lack of harmony in the household. Take care not to suffer as a result of bereavement for elderly relatives. Take caution not to misplace valuables. Damaged or intruders at night
A love horoscope is plenty. During this phase of health, keep an eye out for heart disease, liver illness, diabetes, return of existing ailments, and travel accidents.
In terms of beginning a new career, investing in stocks, and making other decisions. You should think about it thoroughly. Don't merely listen to flattery or utilize short-term rewards to entice

you to do anything. Although there is still a considerable danger in the long term. You must exercise caution before making an investment decision.

Support Days: 3 Mar, 7 Mar., 9 Mar., 11 Mar., 15 Mar., 19 Mar., 23 Mar., 27 Mar., 31 Mar.
Lucky Days: 8 Mar, 20 Mar.
Misfortune Days: 1 Mar, 13 Mar., 25 Mar.
Bad Days: 2 Mar, 4 Mar., 14 Mar., 16 Mar., 26 Mar., 28 Mar.

Month 3 in the Dragon Year (6 Apr 23 - 5 May 23)
As this month begins, your destiny begins to face challenges. Those born in the Year of the Horse are likely to endure challenges and issues throughout the month. Work negotiations will be more difficult than previously. You must maintain your cool in the face of any challenges or disagreements. Don't let your emotions get the best of you. Because it will exacerbate the condition and may reoccur. This month, you should focus on taking care of your tasks as best you can. To resolve problems, do not interrupt and criticize

other people's efforts. This includes arguments among coworkers.

This wage is not excellent in terms of fortune. There is a possibility of losing property in an unforeseen event. Money obtained via fortune-telling entails a significant amount of risk. As a result, don't be too greedy and wind up spending all of your time playing. Furthermore, do not engage in illicit business or copyright infringement since you will most likely be sued. Be careful with your family this month; there will be major disagreements. Family love and peace are more precious than wealth. You should also be concerned about house security. Keep an eye out for misplaced or stolen goods.

Because you are quickly angered and self-centered, you will have difficulties in love. You must maintain good self-control and avoid wandering about at night and causing disputes. However, you will eventually strike the correct balance. Just don't be obnoxious or snarky. In terms of physical health, you will experience sleeplessness, coughing, sore throat, colds, and difficulties eating at this time. This month, you may encounter those who are not serious in their desires for rewards from relatives and friends.

Starting a new job, joining stocks, and making other investments this month will be difficult; thus, investments should be postponed.

Support Days: 4 Apr., 8 Apr., 12 Apr., 16 Apr., 20 Apr., 24 Apr., 28 Apr.

Lucky Days: 1 Apr., 13 Apr., 25 Apr.
Misfortune Days: 6 Apr., 18 Apr., 30 Apr.
Bad Days: 7 Apr., 9 Apr., 19 Apr., 21 Apr.

Month 4 in the Dragon Year (6 May 23 - 5 Jun 23)
The horoscope of people born in the Year of the Horse has shifted to the line of luck this month. You will also receive favorable rays from the dazzling auspicious stars. Increase the strength of your destiny graph to fly. Many unpleasant issues will gradually go away. Work tasks and commercial enterprises will continue to progress. This month, you should analyze your previous mistakes, complete those that are still

outstanding, raise your diligence and develop yourself regularly, expand your knowledge, and dare to make more investments or invest in new topics.

This pay still has a full income, and cash inflows will be plentiful. The harder you work, the more you grow. More chances for riches will arise. You should accelerate your professional growth for your money to expand. In terms of business and commerce, you have the good fortune to find sponsors who can invest in new enterprises, build and launch your store, branch out into product lines, grow branches, and boost product production during this era. Everything will go as planned. There will be fortunate happenings at home and an excellent period for transferring into a new house or business within a happy family.

The romantic aspect is smooth and pleasant. Love's scent is beneficial to moderate physical health. Be wary of joint discomfort, allergies to the air, and reoccurring infections. You should be cautious of mishaps when traveling and maintain good drinking and eating habits. There will be a large number of family and excellent friends who will come to help. Starting a new career, buying stocks, and making other investments are all options. This month seems promising for investing as anticipated.

Support Days: 2 May., 6 May., 10 May., 14 May., 18 May., 22 May., 26 May, and 30 May.
Lucky Days: 7 May., 19 May., 31 May.
Misfortune Days: 12 May., 24 May.
Bad Days: 1 May., 3 May., 13 May., 15 May., 25 May., 27 May.

Month 5 in the Dragon Year (6 Jun 23 - 6 Jul 23)
This month, the path of life for people born in the Year of the Horse has taken a turn for the worse. You will also encounter negative constellations such as the Snaking Star and the Searching Star, which will take control and slow your progress. Work began to face difficulties, and trading was not as easy as it had been in the past. During this time, you should listen to and give special attention to your VIP consumers. Both come in regularly to review the accounts receivable. You should

swiftly follow up and collect from debtors whose debts are past due. Take caution not to fall into bad debt. Those who work frequently throughout this time should be aware that their situation may change. Your manager may reject you if you have not worked hard in the past. Those who do business should be aware that difficulties may develop, and you will be required to clean up the mess that your subordinates produce and inflict harm.

In terms of financial fortune, a monsoon will cause capital to flow out. Do not crave money that you are not entitled to. Because if you want money from other people, you must first spend money. Furthermore, keep in mind that this month's working capital may become stranded and lack liquidity. You should carefully organize your money and avoid gambling and speculating. Do not engage in illicit activities. Beware of people who do not want you good. In terms of the family, keep an eye out for persons in the house who are having mishaps. Because if one person is ill, several others may suffer from a loss of tranquility.

In terms of love, even if everything appears to be going well, you should be wary of those who are tempted to start a fire. It will lead to a fight. You should also avoid going to places of entertainment since this is the same as falling into the trap of flirting with others and establishing a gap in the home.

In terms of health, avoid bronchitis and high blood pressure. You must not drive if you have been drinking. Relatives and friends are not ideal. This month is not a good time to start a new career or make new investments.

Support Days: 3 Jun., 7 Jun., 11 Jun., 15 Jun., 19 Jun., 23 Jun., 27 Jun.
Lucky Days: 12 Jun., 24 Jun.
Misfortune Days: 5 Jun., 17 Jun., 29 Jun
Bad Days: 6 Jun., 8 Jun., 18 Jun., 20 Jun., 30 Jun.

Month 6 in the Dragon Year (7 Jul 23 - 7 Aug 23)
This month, the horoscope of persons born in the Year of the Horse shifts to the alliance line. Along with the fortunate stars' backing, there will be power to support the horoscope's

expected optimistic trajectory. Work will be enjoyable, and business will prosper. As a result, this month, you should demonstrate your talents to the fullest to acquire the trust of your superiors. Both utilize solid ties with others around you to request convenience while dealing with challenging issues. Look for favorable timing while extending work, growing sales, or entering new markets. If you have already planned and prepared, you should rush and turn on the green light to do so quickly. You should strike the iron while the heat is hot throughout this time.

Although the path of improvement is positive for work, particularly commercial companies. But you must not forget to express your thanks to those who assisted you. You must also be friendly with your coworkers. This compensation is still quite high. Please be diligent and continue to grow. The more money you receive, the better. When it comes to spending, however, you should save first. Make it a habit to eliminate unnecessary items. Don't gamble or invest in unlawful enterprises. It is also not permitted to lend money to others or sign financial assurances.

Relationships within the family improved. During this time, the love horoscope is favorable for engagement, marriage, or marriage. In terms of health, avoid gastritis, inflammatory bowel disease, and food poisoning, and be cautious of accidents when working or going outside. This month is favorable for family and friends. If you get stranded, you'll get assistance. It will be a good time to start a new career, buy stocks, and invest in many industries. The money invested will provide excellent returns.

Support Days: 1 Jul., 5 Jul., 9 Jul., 13 Jul., 17 Jul., 21 Jul., 25 Jul., 29 Jul.
Lucky Days: 6 Jul., 18 Jul., 30 Jul
Misfortune Days: 11 Jul., 23 Jul.
Bad Days: 2 Jul., 12 Jul., 14 Jul., 24 Jul., 26 Jul.

Month 7 in the Dragon Year (8 Aug 23 - 7 Sep 23)
This month, the fate criterion for people born in the Year of the Horse will be adjusted to a greater direction than the previous month. Work and business will find support, so please hurry and grasp any good opportunities that come your way. Don't let it pass you by. Hurry and produce more work while increasing your diligence. Find strategies to increase sales and revenue in a variety of sectors. Investing in a new firm, a new trade channel, or growing from something old to something new all have a favorable tendency and will create positive feedback. This month, you should examine market demands to introduce specific items to the market. Anything that addresses a large number of consumer issues will yield a large return.

This compensation is lucrative. Cash inflows will continue. Both from normal money and the chance to get extra money from fortune. What you invest in extra matters will increase significantly. However, you must not be overly thoughtless or greedy. The horoscope of the family has discovered the power of patronage. You may opt to purchase pricey property for the residence at this time. The members of the family live happily together.

Good health, however for seniors, be cautious of heart problems, high blood pressure, and injuries when traveling. People love each other as they please and are willing to assist. This month is favorable for family and friends: they will get guidance to assist them in managing job issues, allowing them to advance from the ranks and become leaders. Starting a new job, investing in stocks, and making other investments this month will all help you make money. Please think about it thoroughly.

Support Days: 2 Aug., 6 Aug., 10 Aug., 14 Aug., 18 Aug., 22 Aug., 26 Aug., 30 Aug
Lucky Days: 11 Aug., 23 Aug.
Misfortune Days: 4 Aug., 16 Aug., 28 Aug
Bad Days: 5 Aug., 7 Aug., 17 Aug., 19 Aug., 29 Aug., 31 Aug.

Month 8 in the Dragon Year (8 Sep 23 - 7 Oct 23)

The fortunes of those born in the Year of the Horse are smooth this month. The life path is heading in a better direction than it was last month. During this period, you should intend to prioritize the effort of reducing vital areas to a bare minimum. Both are searching for methods to modify some work systems to stay up with the circumstances so that work can progress and produce the best outcomes. To cope with this shifting environment, new ways of thinking, new activities, or readjusting oneself may be required. You should also improve your diligence and perseverance. To acquire money to make up for lost revenue in the past. Because the money side of things is looking up this month. Many individuals are rooting for your financial prosperity. As a consequence, you can choose to invest in a variety of firms or make new investments, and you will earn strong returns and be able to progress toward your objectives. In terms of work and business, at this point, diligence in work must be maintained consistently so that results may be obtained uninterrupted. Preparation is still required. When an opportunity presents itself, you will not miss it because there are no items available to please customers since you did not place a reserve.

The fortunes of the family are quite calm and serene. There will be long-distance visitors this month. In terms of health, avoid hand and foot injuries, as well as stomach disorders and food poisoning. The love horoscope has been subjected to winds and seas. Be aware that joking might sometimes lead to suspicion. In terms of family and friends, this month is favorable; you will meet with pals to assist in introducing new clients and handling difficulties. Starting a new career, buying stocks, and making other investments are all options. This month has started to come into place and has a positive trend.

Support Days: 3 Sep., 7 Sep., 11 Sep., 15 Sep., 19 Sep., 23 Sep., 27 Sep.
Lucky Days: 4 Sep., 16 Sep., 28 Sep.
Misfortune Days: 9 Sep., 21 Sep.
Bad Days: 10 Sep., 12 Sep., 22 Sep., 24 Sep.

Month 9 in the Dragon Year (8 Oct 23 - 6 Nov 23)

This month, the fate of people born in the Year of the Horse enters the calm terrain. The auspicious stars will also help you. Assist in the promotion of many sticky issues so that operations may continue to run smoothly. You will have the chance to produce results and make advancements in your career. Trading enterprises will have plenty of opportunities to profit. As a result, this month, you should take the risk of investing in fresh markets with a promising future. You must also be willing to risk expanding your firm, adding items, increasing sales, and increasing revenue. It will help you save money.

Financial fortune, plenty of income, and good financial inflows, whether from a regular wage or sales of goods or services. There will be an infusion of income from extra labor, commissions, or money from fortune. However, you must know how to save for the months when your finances are deteriorating. Found the power of favor and promotion in the workplace. As a result, gold mining is a viable option. The family horoscope is serene. House members are pleased with their children's achievements. Whether it is the progress of labor or the possession of pricey property.

If you locate the appropriate person, you will have a good love horoscope. This month, asking for love will not be turned down. You can only genuinely love and come and leave, but love can never go away. It is also a health requirement to be cautious of accidents when at work and traveling. Take caution not to injure your head, hands, or legs. Relatives get cooperation and aid as well, including the opportunity to go abroad or conduct meritorious work together. Starting a new job, investing in stocks, and making other investments are all great moves.

Support Days: 1 Oct., 5 Oct., 9 Oct., 13 Oct., 17 Oct., 21 Oct., 25 Oct., 29 Oct.
Lucky Days: 10 Oct., 22 Oct.
Misfortune Days: 3 Oct., 15 Oct., 27 Oct.

Bad Days: 4 Oct., 6 Oct., 16 Oct., 18 Oct., 28 Oct., 30 Oct.

Month 10 in the Dragon Year (7 Nov 23 - 6 Dec 23)

This month, persons born in the Year of the Horse will experience half of the good and half of the bad. In terms of financial luck, while there will be a certain amount of income, there will also be unexpected bills that will drain money from your pocket. As a result, to keep the system liquid, you should limit unneeded items and eliminate needless costs this month. Do not gamble, spend money in unlawful commerce, become engaged in corruption, or be greedy to reduce asset loss.

This is not a decent pay. You will be at risk of losing your property. This month, you must be cautious of bad debts in your accounts receivable. Conflicts will arise in the workplace, including commercial enterprises. Customers who change their minds and go elsewhere to use services or buy items should be avoided. As a result, I ask that you execute your job well. Don't become involved in other people's problems. Just doing this will save you a lot of trouble. Due to the finding of both the demonic stars "Buang Sing" and "Kuang Sao" moving in to expand their influence for the family base this month. You and your family members should take care of and monitor the security of your home. Be cautious and mindful of the elderly's health. You should also be cautious about the risks of bereavement for older relatives. Be wary of misplaced valuables. Damaged or stolen items should be avoided, as should subordinates who cause problems.

In terms of health, they are frequently afflicted with colds and flu. After drinking, do not drive and drive cautiously to avoid accidents. The love element remains consistent, with no pros or downsides. Each individual must still keep their relationship. Relatives and friends must still be examined and separated. Be wary of persons who intend to take advantage of you. Starting a new career, buying stocks, and making other investments are all options. Be wary of fraudsters who come in and develop phony enterprises to fool you and cause you to lose money. As a result, you should always consider carefully before acting.

Support Days: 2 Nov., 6 Nov., 10 Nov., 14 Nov., 18 Nov., 22 Nov., 26 Nov., 30 Nov.
Lucky Days: 3 Nov., 15 Nov., 27 Nov.
Misfortune Days: 8 Nov., 20 Nov.
Bad Days: 9 Nov., 11 Nov., 21 Nov., 23 Nov.

Month 11 in the Dragon Year (7 Dec 23 - 5 Jan 24)

The Year of the Horse's life path is rocky and shaking this month. It's because your fate has progressed to the point of malice. As a result, the destiny graph plummeted rapidly. Work, especially business, is similar to being tested and meeting issues and hurdles. Things were introduced one by one. You should avoid interfering with other people's tasks this month. To be safe, you need first to take care of yourself. You should also manage your money and have enough cash in your wallet. Strange tasks, luxury projects, and easy money are considered twice before undertaking them.

Furthermore, if there is a tale, it is not required to be conveyed. Both should be able to communicate well with others. Understand how to be modest and courteous. Do not be arrogant or intimidate less fortunate people.

In terms of fortune, this wage is not favorable. Income began to decline, failing to achieve the objective, and debtors became difficult to collect, with some incurring bad debts. Meanwhile, costs are rising. As a result, you should not gamble or sign financial promises to support anyone at this time. Avoid becoming entangled in criminal activities. Because there is a potential that a lawsuit may be filed.

In terms of jobs, be wary of swindlers and cheats that take advantage of you. Every action is carefully planned to be a trap. Before signing any contract agreements, you should carefully verify the details. In terms of families, be wary of people in the house arguing with each other and pay attention to home safety.

Stormy waves wash over the loving side. You should be able to regulate your emotions properly. Your health is in poor shape during this time. Be wary of heart disease, liver illness, and diabetes. Please maintain proper drinking and eating habits. Starting a new career, investing in stocks, or making other investments this month is risky and should be avoided for the time being.

Support Days: 4 Dec., 8 Dec., 12 Dec., 16 Dec., 20 Dec., 24 Dec., 28 Dec.
Lucky Days: 9 Dec., 21 Dec.
Misfortune Days: 2 Dec., 14 Dec., 26 Dec.
Bad Days: 3 Dec., 5 Dec., 15 Dec., 17 Dec., 27 Dec., 29 Dec.

Amulet for The Year of the Horse
"Tang Xuanzang"

Those born in the Year of the Horse this year should build and worship sacred things. Place "Tang Xuanzang" on your work desk or cash register to beg for His mercy to help safeguard the person of your destiny from all hazards. Prevent the spread of bad luck and evil and aid in the inspiration of prosperity. Increase your power, prosperity, and your family's tranquility and happiness.

A chapter in the Department of Advanced Feng Shui discusses the gods who will come to reside in the mia keng (house of destiny) for the year. They are gods capable of bringing both good and terrible fortune to the god of fate in that year. When this is the case, worship will improve your luck with the gods that visit you on your birthday. As a consequence, it is said to provide the best outcomes and have the most impact on you to rely on the might of that deity to assist and protect you when your destiny is deteriorating. There are misfortunes to ease and stimulate your business to run efficiently. Bring you and your family luck and success.

Those born in the year of the Horse or Mia Keng (horoscope) are under the sign of the Horse. You must take a stand this year. Dare to take the lead and be decisive. To make this year a successful one. Otherwise, everything will come crashing down around you, so keep your head stable. Don't leave everything up to chance. Greed will only cause pain. Concentrate on sticking to the strategy you devised in the middle of the year to prepare for a less favorable start and finish to the year. There are unpredictable ups and downs in terms of fortune. It is tough to develop in love, and you risk becoming engaged in unpleasant news and being the butt of others. Pay special attention to the digestive and circulatory systems in terms of health. If you want to solve an issue, you should surround yourself with sacred things and wear auspicious pendants. "Tang Xuanzang" to beg His Majesty's authority and reputation to assist in the removal of ill luck and to provide bright and successful knowledge in expanding work and business to grow. Be successful in all you desire, and your desires will be granted shortly.

"Tang Xuanzang" whose full name was "Hian Jang Sae Tan," was born in Henan Province, China. He was born a genius. He has been studying Dhamma since he was a child. He was ordained as a monk when he was older. It was well-known for its morals, meditation, and knowledge until it was patronized by the Tang Emperor. Who was the first ruler of the Tang Dynasty? ruler Taizong was a fervent Buddhist. They adore and revere Phra Hian as well. As a result, please make him an adopted brother. Phra Hian Jang is a persevering monk. The mind is set on dedicating one's life to Buddha. By exploring and gathering the core of Buddhism's teachings. Travel from China to India's distant and inhospitable subcontinent. He traveled for 19 years, reaching a distance of more than 50,000 li. He was zealous about spreading Buddhism and collecting the Tripitaka, which benefited religious people all over the world. As a result, he was given the name "Tang Xuanzang," which means "Tripitaka." "Tang Xuanzang" was his Chinese name. "Tang Sam Chang Huab Shi" translates as "The Dhamma Teacher who translated the Tipiṭaka in the Tang Dynasty". Worshiping the Buddha will aid in the removal of all misfortune and sadness, as well as the removal of bullies and the discovery of a bright and handy way. In doing business and performing numerous job activities, I assist in making everything run as smoothly as possible.

Those born in the Year of the Horse should also wear an auspicious pendant. "Tang Xuanzang" wears it around his neck or takes it with him when traveling both near and far from home. Prosperity and growth in commerce and trade are required for the owner of his destiny to be filled with money and auspicious places. The family is pleased all year, which leads to more efficiency and effectiveness, as well as speedier results than ever before.

Good Direction: Northeast, Northwest, and South
Bad Direction: North
Lucky Colors: Red, Pink, Orange, and Green.
Lucky Times: 1100 – 11.59, 13.00 – 14.59, 19.00 – 20.59.
Bad Times: 05.00 – 06.59, 09.00 – 10.59., 23.00 – 00.59

Good Luck For 2024

Made in the USA
Las Vegas, NV
05 January 2024